What was it like in the past...?

At the seaside

Heinemann
LIBRARY

Louise and Richard Spilsbury

www.heinemann.co.uk/library
Visit our website to find out more information about Heinemann Library books.

To order:
☎ Phone 44 (0) 1865 888066
🖹 Send a fax to 44 (0) 1865 314091
🖥 Visit the Heinemann Bookshop at www.heinemann.co.uk/library to browse our catalogue and order online.

First published in Great Britain by Heinemann Library, Halley Court, Jordan Hill, Oxford OX2 8EJ, a division of Reed Educational and Professional Publishing Ltd. Heinemann is a registered trademark of Reed Educational & Professional Publishing Ltd.

OXFORD MELBOURNE AUCKLAND JOHANNESBURG BLANTYRE
GABORONE IBADAN PORTSMOUTH (NH) USA CHICAGO

© Reed Educational and Professional Publishing Ltd 2002
The moral right of the proprietor has been asserted.

Designed by Celia Floyd
Originated by Ambassador Litho Ltd
Printed in Hong Kong/China

ISBN 0 431 14827 9   (hardback)   ISBN 0 431 14837 6   (paperback)

07 06 05 04 03 02   07 06 05 04 03 02
10 9 8 7 6 5 4 3 2   10 9 8 7 6 5 4 3 2 1

British Library Cataloguing in Publication Data
Spilsbury, Louise
   At the Seaside. – (What was it like in the past?)
1. Vacations – History – Juvenile literature
2. Seaside – History – Juvenile literature
I. Title II.Spilsbury, Richard
394.2'.69146

Acknowledgements
Quotation on page 21 from 'Some liked it hot: the British on holiday at home and abroad' by Miriam Akhtar and Steve Humphries, Virgin Publishing Ltd, 2000.
The Publishers would like to thank the following for permission to reproduce photographs:
Bubbles: Lois Joy Thurston 26, Ian West 29; Corbis: 13; Francis Frith Collection: 11, 22; Hulton Archive: 4, 8, 9, 12, 14, 15, 16, 17, 18, 21; Mary Evans: 10; Powerstock: 27, 28; Stone: 5; Topham: 19, 20, 23, 24, 25; Towner Art Gallery and Local Museum: 7; Victoria and Albert Museum: 6.
Cover photograph reproduced with permission of Hulton Archive.

Our thanks to Stuart Copeman for his help in the preparation of this book.
Every effort has been made to contact copyright holders of any material reproduced in this book. Any omissions will be rectified in subsequent printings if notice is given to the Publisher.

Contents

Words printed in **bold letters like these** are explained in the Glossary.

Each **decade** is highlighted on a timeline at the bottom of the page.

Then and now

If you look at a map of the United Kingdom you will see that there is sea all around it. The seaside is the place where the land meets the sea. There are seaside beaches and **resorts** all around the country.

*Since **Victorian** times lots of people have enjoyed visiting the seaside. This picture of a girl playing on the beach was taken in 1890.*

The picture on this page shows a girl at the seaside in 2000. Both the girls on these pages have been building sandcastles and they are both wearing sunhats to keep the sun off their faces.

In this book we will be thinking about the ways visits to the seaside were different in the past.

What differences can you see between this picture and the one on the opposite page?

1900s: At the seaside

What do you wear when you are at the seaside? Around 100 years ago men wore the suits and ties they wore to work. Women wore long dresses and hats. Children also wore their ordinary clothes at the seaside.

This picture was taken in Blackpool in 1903. What do you notice about the clothes everyone is wearing?

In the 1900s people did not spend a lot of time on the beach when they went to the seaside. One of the things they liked to do was walk along the **promenade**. Promenades are special paths by the sea. You can still see promenades in many seaside towns.

The promenade at Eastbourne in 1900.

1900s: Swimming

Around 100 years ago, not many people could swim. Only a few people had bathing costumes. Some people **rented** costumes, or made their own.

In the 1900s bathing costumes were made of fabric that got very heavy when it was wet. Women and girls wore bathing costumes that looked like dresses.

In some places people who could not swim held onto a rope for safety.

Bathing machines in 1901.

Most people changed into their bathing costumes in special huts. These were called **bathing machines**. They had wheels so they could be pulled down close to the sea.

Evelyn Sharp, wrote in a newspaper in 1906: 'People spend half their morning waiting for a bathing machine, and the other half, five minutes subtracted for a bathe, in dressing themselves with numbed fingers.'

1910s: Piers and amusements

Many seaside towns at this time had **piers**. Piers were like bridges that stopped in the sea. People liked to walk out over the water. Many piers had buildings. These were used for concerts, dances or games.

*This **postcard** shows Weston-Super-Mare pier in 1912. People still send postcards to their friends when they go on holiday.*

People used to listen to bands playing music on the promenade.

People liked to visit seaside towns that had **amusements** on the piers or **promenades**. They liked to watch magic shows and funny shows.

People also liked to buy souvenirs from stalls. Souvenirs are small presents you buy for yourself or your family to remind you of your holiday.

1920s: Healthy outdoors

In the 1920s doctors were telling people to get outdoors more. Many more people began to visit the seaside to enjoy the fresh air. The old bathing costumes were heavy and hard to swim in. The new bathing costumes of this time looked more like the ones we wear today.

It was easier to swim and run and play in the new bathing costumes of the 1920s.

Seaside towns became even busier. Lots of people stayed in boarding houses. These were big houses where you could **rent** a room. Women called landladies looked after these houses. Families bought food for the landladies to cook for their tea.

Seaside towns were very popular in the 1920s.

1930s: Getting to the seaside

Railway lines had been built to some seaside towns in the **Victorian** times. In the 1930s most people still travelled to the seaside by **steam train** because not many families had their own cars. Also, going by steam train was an exciting start to the summer holiday.

In the 1930s you wore your smartest clothes when you went on your holidays by train.

Some people went to quieter beaches by bus or bike or they walked. These beaches were often almost empty, so children had lots of space to play.

Beryl Stewart recalls beach trips in the 1930s: 'Mum, dad and we five children used to walk to Thurlestone, 3 miles away... There was no traffic on the roads. The beaches were almost empty too.'

Beaches like Thurlestone Sands were often empty in the 1930s.

1930s: Young and old

In the 1930s older people still wore their ordinary clothes to the seaside. Many did not even go down to the sand. Some people liked to **rent** deckchairs. They sat in rows on the **promenade** above the beach.

You could rent a deckchair for an hour, an afternoon or even for the whole day.

There were lots of things for children to do on and off the sand. They could have donkey rides, visit the funfair or a **Punch and Judy** show. The small Punch and Judy show tents could be carried from beach to beach. The show could be done anywhere.

These children are enjoying a Punch and Judy show in South Shields in 1930.

1940s: War and peace

From 1939 until 1945 the United Kingdom was at war against Germany. People feared that enemy soldiers would get into the country from the sea. Many of the beaches in the south and east of England were closed. Some beaches were covered in special fences to stop enemy soldiers coming ashore.

In the war, this beach in Bournemouth had long fences to stop enemy soldiers landing at the seaside.

After the war, people were glad to be able to go on holiday again. When the soldiers came home, families could enjoy themselves at last. Seaside towns became busier than ever.

*In the 1940s seaside **resorts** were very busy. Lots of people went to the funfairs by the beaches.*

1950s: Group holidays

Who do you go on holiday with? Today, most families go on holiday by themselves. In the past, many people went on holiday in big groups.

In the 1950s many families took grandparents, aunts, uncles and cousins on holiday with them. Sometimes a group of people from the same street went on holiday together.

In the past, people liked to go to the seaside in big groups.

1900 1910 1920 1930 1940

In the 1950s some **factories** closed for one week in summer. This meant that most of the people in a town went on holiday at the same time, and usually to the same place.

'We rushed home from work on Friday, had a quick wash, and then headed down to the railway station. When we left it was like a ghost town; there was barely a shop open.'

George Wray, a factory worker in the 1950s.

Lots of factory workers in the north of England went to Blackpool.

1960s: Going it alone

Up until this time, most people travelled to their holidays by train. In the 1960s more people owned their own cars. This meant that they could visit quieter beaches away from the seaside towns. Families began to go on holiday on their own, instead of in groups.

There was not room in a car for a lot of people. Families began to go to the seaside by themselves.

When people visited areas far away from the big seaside towns there were fewer places to stay. Some people went camping or stayed in a caravan instead. It was cheaper to camp and people could go where they liked. Instead of visiting the same **resort** every year, people began to visit different beaches.

In the 1960s people who had cars and caravans could visit different places for their seaside holidays.

1970s and 1980s: Flying away

By the 1970s people could fly on big jet planes to other countries for their holidays. People started to take 'package holidays' to sunny places. They were called 'package' holidays because they offered people a whole package – the trip on the aeroplane, a hotel to stay in and meals.

Some people fly to other countries for their seaside holidays.

Holidaymakers on a beach in Spain.

One reason people go to other countries for their seaside holidays is the weather. In Britain, even in summer, it often rains or it is too cold or windy to play on the beach. Some people travel to countries where they know it will be sunny for their holidays.

1990s: Seaside safety

Most people who visit the seaside today know that too much sun can be bad for you. They stay out of the sun at lunchtime because this is the hottest part of the day. People wear sunhats and sunglasses to protect their eyes. They also rub on sun cream to stop the sun hurting their skin.

Some children wear special clothes that stop the sun burning their skin.

There have been **lifeguards** on beaches for over 100 years. Their job is to check that people keep safe. They put coloured flags on some beaches to tell us where to swim. Lifeguards also help people if they swim out too far or get into trouble in the water.

Lifeguards make sure people are safe in the water.

2000s: Seaside fun

In the 100 years between 1900 and 2000 many things changed. In 1900 most children had never sat inside a car, did not have electric lights in their homes and had few toys.

Today we have computers and toys that children of the past could not even have imagined. Yet at the seaside people enjoy doing many of the same things today as they did back then.

Do you like paddling in the sea?

Today, just as in the past, people catch fish and crabs from rock pools with simple nets. People still build sandcastles using buckets and spades. Next time you go to the seaside, think about what things are different to the way they were in the past and what things are the same.

The fun of catching crabs from a rock pool is the same now as it was 100 years ago!

Find out for yourself

You could ask your parents or grandparents what they used to do and where they used to go on holiday. You could also ask if they have any old photographs that you can look at.

Lots of seaside towns have museums you could visit. You can also look in the library and bookshops for books about the seaside. Here are some books you might like to read.

Books

Fifty years ago: Going on a trip, Hodder Wayland, 1998

History from photographs: Journeys, Hodder Wayland, 1999

What was it like in the Past? On journeys, Heinemann Library, 2002

Glossary

amusements games and shows that amuse people. 'Amuse' means making someone happy.

bathing machines huts on wheels that people went in to put their bathing costumes on

decade ten years. The decade of the 1910s means the ten years between 1910 and 1920.

factories very big buildings where people use machines to make things, such as cars or toys

lifeguards special people who make sure that other people keep safe in the water

piers these look like bridges that stop a little way out to sea

postcards pictures on card which you send to people to show them where you are on holiday

promenades special paths by the sea in seaside towns

Punch and Judy show puppet show about a man and wife, called Punch and Judy, who have funny fights

rent when you pay money to use something for a little while

resorts towns by the sea which lots of people visit for their holidays

steam train trains powered by coal. The coal was burned in hot fires and made lots of smoke and steam.

Victorians people who lived when Victoria was Queen of England (from 1837 until 1901)

Index

Titles in the *What was it like in the past...?* series include:

Hardback   0 431 14826 0

Hardback   0 431 14828 7

Hardback   0 431 14827 9

Hardback   0 431 14821 X

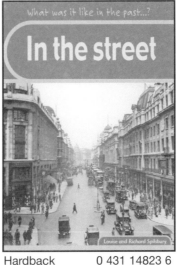

Hardback   0 431 14823 6

Hardback   0 431 14825 2

Hardback   0 431 14822 8

Hardback   0 431 14820 1

Find out about the other titles in this series on our website www.heinemann.co.uk/library